D1084218

A Day With Daddy

Written by Louise A. Gikow

Illustrated by Gustavo Mazali

children's press®

A Division of Scholastic Inc.

New York Toronto London Auckland Sydney
Mexico City New Delhi Hong Kong
Danbury, Connecticut

Library of Congress Cataloging-in-Publication Data

Gikow, Louise.
  A day with Daddy / written by Louise A. Gikow ; illustrated by Gustavo
Mazali.
      p. cm. – (My first reader)
Summary: After a visit to the zoo with the children, it is Daddy who
needs the nap.
  ISBN 0-516-24410-8 (lib. bdg.)   0-516-25501-0 (pbk.)
  [1. Fathers and children–Fiction. 2. Zoos–Fiction. 3. Naps
(Sleep)–Fiction. 4. Stories in rhyme.] I. Mazali, Gustavo, ill. II.
Title. III. Series.
  PZ8.3.G376Da 2004
  [E]–dc22
                                        2003015919

Published in 2004 by Children's Press, an imprint of Scholastic Library Publishing.
Published simultaneously in Canada.
Printed in the United States of America.

CHILDREN'S PRESS and associated logos are trademarks and or
registered trademarks of Scholastic Library Publishing. SCHOLASTIC and
associated logos are trademarks and or registered trademarks of Scholastic Inc.

1 2 3 4 5 6 7 8 9 10 R 13 12 11 10 09 08 07 06 05 04

Note to Parents and Teachers

Once a reader can recognize and identify the 48 words
used to tell this story, he or she will be able to successfully
read the entire book. These 48 words are repeated throughout
the story, so that young readers will be able to recognize
the words easily and understand their meaning.

The 48 words used in this book are:

and	eat	know	seals	too
are	feet	look	sky	top
at	go	me	sleepy	up
best	hang	monkeys	slow	want
by	he	on	stop	wants
come	help	our	ten	we
count	hide	pick	the	what
daddy	high	push	their	you
do	I	rest	they	
down	is	ride	to	

Come on, Daddy, we want to go!

Come on, Daddy, you are too slow!

Look at the monkeys
hang by their feet!

Look at the seals!

They want to eat!

Come on, Daddy, we want to eat, too.

Come on, Daddy, we know what to do!

Push me, Daddy, I want to go high.

Push me, push me up to the sky!

I want to go up, up, up to the top.

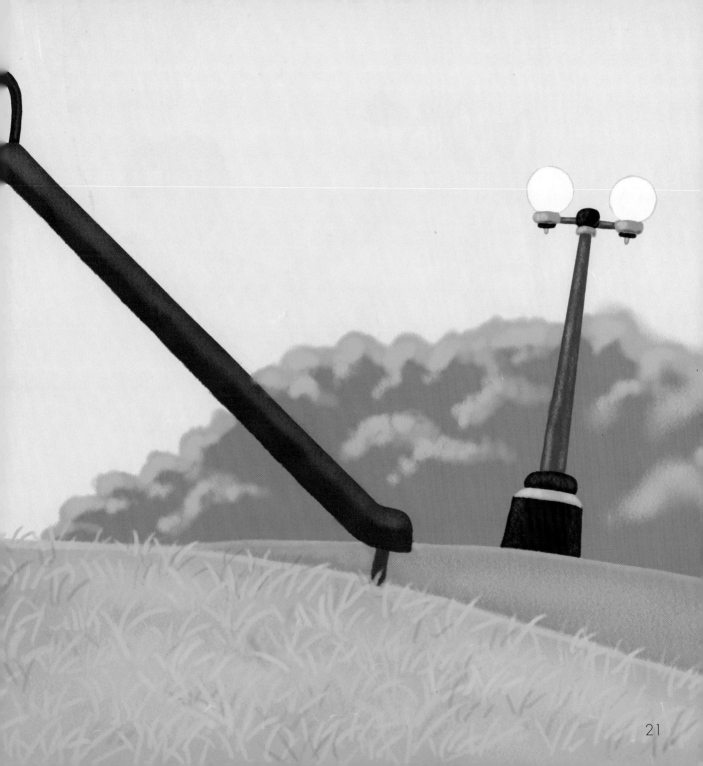

I want to go down, Daddy.

Help me stop!

Count to ten, Daddy,
we want to hide.

Pick me up, Daddy, I want to ride.

Daddy is sleepy,
and he wants to rest.

He is our Daddy. He is the best!

ABOUT THE AUTHOR

Louise A. Gikow has written hundreds of books for children (and a few for young adults and grown-ups, too). She was inspired to write *A Day With Daddy* because of the memories she has of her own father. Gikow has also written songs and scripts for videos and television shows. Most recently, she was a writer for *Between the Lions,* the PBS-Kids TV series that helps children learn to read.

ABOUT THE ILLUSTRATOR

Gustavo Mazali has been drawing since he was a little boy in the 1960s. When he grew up, he started illustrating comics. He then began illustrating children's books, which he loves doing. Mazali lives in Buenos Aires, Argentina, with his wife and children, who are his inspiration.